THE SECRET LIFE OF BEER

LEGENDS, LORE & LITTLE-KNOWN FACTS

ALAN D. EAMES

Storey Publishing

*The mission of Storey Publishing is to serve our customers
by publishing practical information that encourages personal
independence in harmony with the environment.*

Cover and text design by Carol Jessop
Cover and interior art by Danny O
Copyright © 2004 Alan D. Eames

The information in this book is true and complete to the best of our knowledge. All
recommendations are made without guarantee on the part of the author or Storey
Publishing. The author and publisher disclaim any liability in connection with the use of
this information. For additional information please contact Storey Publishing, 210 MASS
MoCA Way, North Adams, MA 01247.

Storey books are available for special premium and promotional uses and for
customized editions. For further information, please call 1-800-793-9396.

Printed in the United States by Von Hoffmann
10 9 8 7 6 5 4 3 2 1

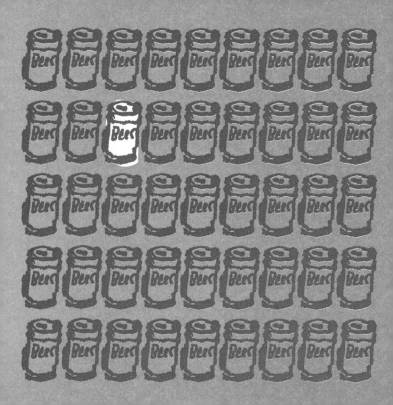

Mankind: The animal that
fears the future and
desires fermented beverages.

Anthelme Brillat-Savarin
(1755-1826)

The Pharoah's charter of 2300 BC states that Osiris founded the dynasty of the Beer Kings.

Bes, the ancient Egyptian goddess of childbirth, was also known for her fondness for beer. Often portrayed as a dwarf with no clear gender distinction, Bes's spiritual association with brewing was second only to that of the goddess Hathor.

In Peru I watched three Quechua crones bustle about the boiling beer pots. They hovered over the brew-kettles exhorting the corn goddess, Mamasara, to work her magic into the chicha. The women worked with no electricity, in an eerie, candle-lit, foul-smelling hovel with bleeding, eviscerated animal corpses hanging from the rafters. The entire room was filled with bubbling beer cauldrons, like some dark medieval nightmare. I asked the women, "Do men ever make the beer?" My question was met with gales of raucous laughter. "Men can't brew! Chicha made by men only makes gas in the belly. You are a funny man, beer is woman's work."

Ancestral women maintained power and status in a male dominated society through their skills as brewers.

A BEER DRINKER'S COMPANION

Ale is rightly called nappy, for it will set a nap upon a man's threadbare eyes when he is sleepy. It is called merry-go-downe, for it slides down merrily. It is fragrant to the scent; it is most pleasant to the taste; it is delightful to the sight; it is touching or feeling to the brain and heart;...it provokes men to singing and mirth...The taking of it doth comfort the heavy and troubled mind...it is the warmest lining of a naked man's coat; it satiates and assuages hunger and cold; with a toast it is the poor man's comfort; the...plowman's most esteemed pur-

chaser; it is the tinker's treasure, the
peddlar's jewel, the beggar's joy, and
the prisoner's loving nurse;...it will
set a bashful suitor wooing; it heats
the chilled blood of the aged;...it is a
friend to the muses; it inspires the
poor poet...it puts eloquence into the
oratour, it will make the philosopher
talk profoundly, the scholar learnedly,
and the lawyer...feelingly...It is a
great friend to the truth...it is an
emblem of justice... it will put courage
into a coward... it is a seal to a bar-
gain; the physician will commend it; the
lawyer will defend it; it hurts nor
kills any but those who abuse it...it is
the nourisher of mankind.

John Taylor, 1580-1653

Gimme a pigfoot
and a bottle of
beer.

Besse Smith (1894-1937),
American Blues singer

BEER AND THE GODDESS

Beer is a gift from the goddesses, a soothing balm given our species to bring joy and comfort in compensation for the curse of self-awareness, the awful realization of our mortality. Beer — nourisher and liquid bread, inspirer of song and story, tribal tale-teller, mother and father of democracy — its domestication led to civilization itself. Beer is the stuff of our species and is in our very blood and bones.

BEER IS BORN

Ten, twenty, perhaps fifty thousand years ago a woman hunter-gatherer with a gourd of grain was caught in a torrential downpour. Fleeing the lightning and thunder, the woman left the drenched seeds behind as she scurried for cover. The sun reappeared as ambient yeast infected the bowl of abandoned, fermenting gruel. Bubbling and sudsing, the world's first brew waited for perhaps another woman to come along and spy the concoction. A curious sip followed by a grunt of pleasure at the tart taste followed by a deeper swig. Soon a strange sensa-

tion took hold of the woman. Dizzy,
lightheaded feelings gave way to
drunkenness — and beer was born.

Whoever makes a poor beer is transferred to the dung-hill.

Edict, City of Danzig, 11th century

BEER ETIQUETTE

In Munich patrons of hofbrau houses rinsed their own mugs in a trough before taking them to the bar to be refilled.

When the chill northeast wind blows,
And winter tells a heavy tale,
When pyes and dawes and doobes and
  crowes
Do sit and curse the frostes and
  snowes,
Then give me ale.

                  16th century English verse

The English hop plant is a species of morning glory, several varieties of which contain hallucinogenic properties.

BEER AND SONG

He that buys land buys many stones,
He that buys flesh buys many bones,
He that buys eggs buys many shells,
But he that buys good ale buys
  nothing else.

English Medieval song

THE PHILOSOPHICAL DRINKER

Kindly observe the tankard of beer I offer you. This book was not made simply to drink. It was made to speak to you. And if you, with your tankard of beer, could learn the dialogue, you would discover that in your tankard lives a milky way of tiny bubbles. And inside each bubble, there exists an idea that is waiting to be discovered. Each one of these ideas can make you grand and large and fortunate if you so desire to learn to talk with beer.

M. Bellot

A LITERARY BREW

...he would go for a ride on the
Third Avenue "E." It would please him
to see the four enormous, beautifully
polished copper kettles in the windows
of Ruppert's brewery, and it would
please him to smell the wet hops, a
lovely smell that blew into the car
as it rattled past.

Joseph Mitchell, <u>The Lost Weekend</u>

I know Bacchus, the
god of wine, for he
smells of nectar;
but all I know of
the god of beer is
that he smells of
the billy goat.

Emperor Julian the Apostate,
361 A.D.

In the folktales of tribal Africa, a black Pandora repeats her Greek sister's rash act except the African makes a different discovery remaining in the casket. Not hope...but rather, a gourd of beer.

...Man's first civilization gave great place to intoxication. Long before there was decadence or world-weariness, men and women wanted to change their response to the planet on which they had evolved to self-consciousness.

Jacquetta Hawkes,
The First Great Civilizations

In all ancient societies, in the religious mythologies of all ancient cultures, beer was a gift to women from a goddess, never a male god, and women remained bonded in complex religious relationships with feminine deities who blessed the brew vessels.

BEER AND THE GODDESS

The ancient legends tell how the goddess took pity on the miserable plight of humanity and so loved her daughters that she bestowed the gift of beer to their sole keeping. Twenty thousand years ago, it was a goddess who gave life and abundance and it was the goddess who, out of a mother's love and pity for her fallen children, gave the gift of brew to the women of mankind. The cup of bliss, the gourd of temporary forgetfulness was filled with beer.

No children
without sex —
no drunkenness
without beer.

Ancient Sumerian proverb

For early mankind, the mood-altering properties of beer were supernatural. The newfound state of intoxication was considered divine. Beer, it was thought, must contain a spirit or god, since the drinking of the liquid so possessed the spirit of the drinker.

For we could not now take time for
further search (to land our ship),
our victuals being much spent,
especially our beer.

Log, The Mayflower

BEER AND WOMEN

Brewsters quickly became priest-esses and without beer, no one could commune with the goddess. Women oversaw the collective drinking of beer acting as barmaids and bouncers enforcing rules of conduct while ensuring men didn't injure themselves. Beer-drunken elder men became story-tellers reciting the tribal tales and histories. When the elders were in their cups, the women would awaken the children to sit and listen around the fires and in this regard beer became the single most important aspect in learning among preliterate cultures.

The immense importance
of a pint of ale to a
common person should
never be overlooked.

Canon of St. Paul's Cathedral,
18th century

Some anthropologists suggest ceramics, such as clay pots and vessels, were created for the sole purpose of fermenting and storing beer.

Brehm asserts that the natives of Northeastern Africa catch the wild baboons by exposing vessels with strong beer, by which they are made drunk...On the following morning they [the baboons] were very cross and dismal; they held their aching heads with both hands.

Charles Darwin,
The Origin of Species, 1859

The process of fermentation increases fourfold the vitamin and mineral content of plain seeds or grains. Ambient yeast adds additional and substantial levels of protein and vitamins B and C.

In nature, when rainwater meets grain, the seeds begin to sprout. Sprouting causes a natural conversion of starch into fermentable sugar. With time, women discovered that beer could be brewed stronger and faster if the cereals were chewed before adding them to water, because the enzyme pytalin (found in saliva) converts cereal starch into fermentable sugar.

BEER AND SONG

The wonderful love of a beautiful
  young maid...
The love of a staunch true man,
The love of a baby unafraid,
All have existed since time began.
But the greatest love — the love of
  all loves,
Even greater than that of a mother...
Is the tender, passionate, undying
  love,
of one beer-drunken slob for another.

                                    Anonymous

Beer bouts were the site of the first schools of higher learning. Before reading and writing all tribal wisdom was passed from one generation to the next over a pot of beer.

By adding chewed mash to the beer pot, higher sugar levels created more bang to the gourd full of the local Stone-Age beer. Honey, combs and all, was an additional source of fermentable sugar. This, the oldest method of beer making, is still practiced in remote areas throughout the world.

Of beer
an enthusiast has
said that it could
never be bad, but
that some brands
might be better than
others...

A.A. Milne (1882-1956)

A BREW A DAY...

At a time before bread baking, beer was a non-perishable food. Protected by alcohol, beer had a palatability lasting far longer than any other foodstuff. A vitamin-rich porridge, beer, used daily, is reported to have increased health and longevity, and reduced disease and malnutrition.

I feel wonderful
drinking beer;
in a blissful
mood with joy
in my heart and
a happy liver.

Sumerian poet, circa 3000 B.C.

The government that increases the price of beer cannot last longer than the next plum harvest.

Czechoslovakian homily

Ten thousand years ago barley was domesticated and worshipped as a God in the highlands of the southern Levant. Thus, beer was the driving force that led nomadic mankind into village life. With the creation of writing — stylus on wet clay tablet — beer, its history and mystery, became a large part of ancient man's literary repertoire.

Ama-Gestin, the Earth Mother, and Ninkasi, the lady who fills the mouth, were the goddesses of beer in the ancient world.

May Ninkasi live with you —
  let her pour your beer
  everlasting.
My sister, your grain — its
  beer is tasty, my comfort.

Sumerian greetings

BEER AND WOMEN

The women of ancient Sumeria brewed and sold beer, and ran taverns under the spiritual protection of Siduri, goddess of the brewery and patroness of wisdom. The dominance of women in the brewing arts appears time and again in cuneiform poem and prayer.

Sabtiem, women brewsters and tavern keepers, were the only tradespeople of their era with private deities who spiritually guided the making of a bewildering number of beers. "Black and White Beer," "Beer of Two Parts," "Beer from the World Below," "Beer of Sacrifice," "Supper Beer," "Horned Beer," "Wheat Beer," and the apparently foamy "Beer With a Head."

For our food,
I slaughtered
sheep and oxen,
day by day; with
beer, oil and
water, I filled
large jars.

Atrahasis, ancient Sumerian folk hero

Among the myths of Sumeria was the precursor of the Christian tale of Noah and the flood. The Noah of Sumeria was Atrahasis, who brought beer aboard his ark when told by God that mankind was to be drowned for being too noisy.

Beer shops, called Bit Sikari, and taverns were common in Sumerian cities and villages. As drunkenness was a spiritual state, beery transactions were not to be sullied by the exchange of money. In the Code of Hammurabi the sale of beer for silver or gold was forbidden.

If a beer seller do not receive barley as the price of beer, but if she receive money...or make the beer measure smaller than the barley measure received, they (the judges) shall throw her (the brewster) into the water.

Code of Hammurabi 1500-2000 B.C.

Beer he drank — seven goblets.
His spirit was loosened. He became
hilarious. His heart was glad and
his face shone.

> Epic of Gilgamesh, the oldest
> narrative tale, circa 3000 B.C.

Those who drank deeply and daily thrived as the search continued for new sources of grain to make beer. It was this appetite for beer-making material that may have led to crop cultivation, settlements, and agriculture.

Archaeological sites throughout the Tigris-Euphrates region have yielded thousands of cuneiform tablets containing recipes for, and prayers in praise of, beer. "Kassi — black beer," "Kassag — fine black beer," "Kassagasaan — finest premium beer," and "Kassig — red beer" were not only savored as beverages, but also formed the basis for most medicinal remedies for ailments, from scorpion stings to heart conditions.

Every human culture that enjoyed beer seems to have been balanced by a vocal minority that viewed malt beverages as a threat to public morals.

BEER AND WOMEN

While priestesses were forced to drink in secret, the use of attractive bare-breasted women, for the purpose of advertising beer brands and beer shops, was in vogue in ancient Sumeria. Carved in high relief, images of curvaceous barmaids invited patrons to sample the delights of beer, and sometimes brothel.

The combination of sexuality and beer, in the form of advertising, lured the tired and thirsty into the local beer shop, beginning a trend that would survive the rise and fall of many civilizations.

Social sanctions prohibited high priestesses from loitering in beer halls under penalty of death by burning.

Oh Lord thou shalt not
enter the beer shop!
The beer drunkard shall
soak your gown with vomit.

Cuneiform tablets
from the Tigris-Euphrates region

Despite Draconian restrictions for the few, beer endured as a joyful part of life. Drinking songs, sung by all classes, reflect the happiness provided by time in the beer halls.

BEER AND SONG

The Gakkul vat, the Gakkul vat,
  [fermenting vessel]
The Gakkul, the Lamsare vat,
The Gakkul vat, which makes
  the liver happy,
The Lamsare vat, which
  rejoices the heart,
The Urgurbal jar, a good
  thing in the house,
The Sagub jar, which is
  filled with beer...
The beautiful vessels are
  ready on their stands!

            Song from Ancient Sumeria

A cuneiform tablet from the Tigris-Euphrates region, perhaps the oldest beer advertisement, encourages patrons to "Drink Ebla — the beer with the heart of a lion."

Who fed you on the food of the god?
Who gave you beer to drink, fit for
  kings...Let sweet beer flow through
  thy straw,
Their bodies swell as they drink.

                              Epic of Gilgamesh

Let a neat housewife
...have the handling
of good ingredients
— sweet malt and
good water — and you
shall see and will
say there is an art
in brewing.

Dr. Cyril Folkingham, 1623

BEER'S BEGINNINGS

The Egyptian goddess Hathor, while trying to destroy mankind, inadvertently invented beer. Hathor survived the entire dynastic ages as Queen of drunkenness, dance, and beer.

HOW HATHOR BECAME THE CHIEF GODDESS OF BEER

A time came when the Sun God Re lost his divine patience with mankind. Re saw his temples neglected, his subjects fornicating, fighting, lying, stealing, and worse. Deciding to punish his children, Re gave the task to the goddess Hathor, women being so much better at enforcement than men. While Re turned his divine attention to other things, Hathor took the form of a leopardess and descended to Earth.

At the end of the first day of punishment, Re looked to see how Hathor was doing. To his horror, he saw the streets of Egypt running red with blood. A handful of humans survived. Having given Hathor three days of divine punishment duty, Re could not now stop her. He threw sweet dates and barley into the human blood that covered the land.

The sun arose the next day and the mixture of blood, barley, and dates fermented. Beer was born. Hathor awoke planning to hunt the few remaining Egyptians, but she smelled the odor of beer. She tentatively lapped at the brew. She found the beer so pleasing that she drank herself into a stupor and drunkenly snored for two days and nights. Upon awakening, the goddess found her time was up. Beer was created, the human species was saved, and Hathor became Goddess of Beer.

In this year, about
the Feast of John
the Baptist, our ale
failed.

Church records,
Dunstable, England, 1262

The ancient Egyptians were obsessed with beer — it anointed the newborn baby, was minimum wage for a day's work, and went into the tomb with the dead. The Nile dwellers even wrote the word 'food' as a loaf of bread and a pitcher of beer.

Non-alcoholic beers came from old Egypt. Egyptian priestesses would brew a potent beer that was taken into the temple and heated over fire, the alcohol or 'spirit' of the beer rising to heaven and making the goddess quite drunk. The remaining, now non-alcoholic brew was sold to the public, the proceeds going to support the temple.

THE BEER
GODDESS'S PRAYER

"We soothe your majesty daily (with
  offerings of beer),
Your heart rejoices when you hear our
  song.
Our hearts exult at a glance of your
  majesty.
You are queen of the wreath
The queen of dance
The queen of drunkenness without end."

ORIGIN OF ALE

According to the "Kalevala," the story and song cycle of the ancient Finnish people, beer was born through the efforts of three women preparing for a wedding feast: Osmotar, Kapo, and Kalevatar. Their first efforts fell as flat as the brew they were trying to create. It was only when Kalevatar combined saliva from a bear's mouth with wild honey that the beer foamed and the gift of ale came into the world.

BEER'S BEGINNINGS

Osmotar placed the honey in the
  liquor
And the wedding-beer fermented;
Rose the live beer upward, upward,
From the bottom of the vessels,
Upward in the tubs of birch-wood,
Foaming higher, higher, higher,
Till it touched the oaken handles,
Thus was brewed the beer of
  Northland,
At the hands of Osmotar;
This the origin of brewing.

Great indeed the reputation of the
    ancient beer —
Said to make the feeble hardy,
Famed to dry the tears of women,
Famed to cheer the broken-hearted,
Make the timid brave and mighty,
Fill the heart with joy and gladness,
Fill the mind with wisdom,
Fill the tongue with ancient legends,
Only makes the fool more foolish.

    Kalevala, Rune #20, translated from
        Peter Borne Missza's 1578 edition

For Egyptians, beer drinking was something gods and goddesses did daily. The libation cup — the ritual cup of milk, honey, wine, or most often, beer — would be poured over a statue of the god.

**Beer drinkin'
don't do half
the harm as
love makin'.**

Ancient wisdom

Do not cease to drink beer,
to eat, to intoxicate
thyself,
to make love and
celebrate
the good days.

Egyptian saying

(I recommend)...
bread, meat,
vegetables and
beer.

Sophocles (circa 496-406 B.C.)

BEER'S BEGINNINGS

Zosimus, a 5th century chemist, described the Egyptian brewing process:

"Take fine, clean barley and moisten it for one day; then draw it off and lay it up on a windless place until morning...again wet it and dry it...until shredded...and rub it until it falls apart. Next, grind it and make it into loaves...just like bread, and cook it rather raw, and when the loaves rise, dissolve sweet water and strain through a sieve."

These half-baked loaves were mashed
and crumbled then forced through the
bottom of a woven reed basket — the
mixed liquid falling into a large fermenting jar below. These clay jars,
most larger than a man, were covered
on the outside with pitch to make them
airtight. When filled with beer, the
fermenting jar was then stoppered with
a plug of Nile mud and lagering began.

Fermentation and civilization are inseparable.

John Ciardi (1916-1986)

Every household in ancient Egypt, rich or poor, brewed beer. For the average family, the household brewery was located in the part of the kitchen called the "pure." Most often women were responsible for brewing and selling beer; both in the home and in Egypt's many beer shops.

And thou shalt give to me
to eat until I am satis-
fied, and thou shalt give
to me beer until I am
drunk. And thou shalt
establish my issue as
kings, forever and ever.

Ramses IV, circa 1200 B.C.

The palace of the Pharaoh provided the royal household with its own regal brews; the office of Chief Beer Inspector being responsible for quality control.

In ancient Egypt beer was money; the minimum wage of the day being two pitchers, each several gallons in size, per day's work. The Pharaoh received thousands of jars of beer each year in the form of taxes and tribute from cities, provinces, and territories.

...it is only those who get
drunk on beer who fall on
their backs and lie with
their faces upwards.

Aristotle (384-322 B.C.)

Greek physician Dioskorides complained that Egyptian beer caused too frequent urination and the Greeks feared that beer caused leprosy.

The Egyptian brew "zythos" was imported by the shipload into Mediterranean ports for use by craftsmen to soften ivory in the manufacture of jewelry.

Egyptian beers all had a degree of sweetness. Bittering agents, herbs, and the like, were not included in the brew, but were served with the beer as a condiment. Patrons of an ancient beer shop were offered platters of dry twists of skirret, a bitter plant. The drinker placed these herbal plugs between the cheek and gum. The skirret provided a pleasant bitter flavoring as the sweet beer entered the mouth.

The Egyptians make the sweet taste of their beer palatable by adding to it pungent spices and lupine.

Columella, Rome, 1st century A.D.

BEER AND WOMEN

In hidden, remote places around the world from the jungles of South America to the steppes of Asia, women still hold close the arts of brewing. Praying to their ancient goddesses, the women of non-technological societies continue to pass down to their daughters the secrets of beer. The old ways have not gone but soon will be.

The mouth of
the perfectly
happy man is
filled with
beer.

Egypt's multi-dynasty slogan

BEER ETIQUETTE

When calling at a friend's house or entering a beer shop, a visitor would be greeted by a servant carrying a small wooden corpse in a casket. Holding the gruesome icon under the guest's nose, the host would intone words to the effect of: "See here? Soon this is how you shall be. So drink deep and enjoy thyself." Formalities over, the beery evening began.

For Egyptians, being drunk was being spiritual. Respectable Egyptians would give their children socially acceptable names like: "How Drunk is Cheops," or "How Intoxicated is Hathor."

Don't undertake
to drink a whole
pitcher of beer.
Because if you
then talk, from
your mouth comes
nonsense..."

Papyrus Anastasi IV

HAIR OF THE DOG

The hangover, which intoxicated Egyptians called "the pulling of the hair," was of top priority to the ancient medical community. Cabbage juice was a Pharaoh's first line of defense against beery over-indulgence. For hundreds of years, the modern world has recorded the ancient Egyptian cabbage remedy with great amusement. However recent scientific research has discovered that cabbage contains chelators which are effective in neutralizing acetaldehydes, a most unpleasant by-product of our livers' efforts to metabolize alcohol.

Wife, quick!
Some cabbage
boil, of virtu-
ous healing,
that I may rid
me of this
seedy feeling.

Eubulus, ancient author
(circa 405-335 B.C.)

Last evening you were beer-
drinking deep, so now your
head aches. Go to sleep.
Take some boiled cabbage
and when you wake, there's
end of your headache.

Athenaeus (2nd century)

BEER DREAMS

To even dream of beer was significant
enough to the Egyptians that by the
19th Dynasty (1306 B.C.), an entire
volume appeared explaining the meaning
of beer-dream symbols.

When he dreams of sweet beer, he will
  become happy.

When he dreams of bakery beer, he
  will live.

When he dreams of cellar beer, he
  shall have security.

Wine is but
single broth,
ale is meat,
drink, and
cloth.

16th century English proverb

THE DRINKING AGE

The Aztecs forbade drunkenness except among those who were 52 years of age and older.

The Aztecs believed a drunken person was under the influence of a spirit or god, represented in the form of a rabbit — a creature considered by the Aztecs to have no sense at all. Chief among the rabbit-drunk deities was Ometochtli. Anyone born on the "two rabbit" day of the drink god Tepoxtecatl was believed doomed to be a hopeless drunk.

Prayer to the spirits of the corn or manioc further strengthens the beer. During the night, a circle of bows and arrows ring the beer pots to further ward away the souls of the dead.

Drunk I was, I was over drunk.

The Norse God Odin, The Havamal Saga

BEER AND SONG

Then a
bottle of
melodius
beer, if you please,
with a few chromatic
splinters in it.

A.E. Coppard,
Fishmonger's Fiddle

BEER IN CENTRAL AMERICA

In pre-Columbian Mesoamerica, the Aztecs brewed a chicha-like brew called sendecho from corn and bittered the brew with the plant tepozan. Early Spanish explorers commented on the exceptional strength of another Aztec beer-like beverage called tesguino.

ALE AND THE VIKINGS

Ale was perhaps the most important item in Viking life. The Vikings were the terror of the 8th through 10th centuries. Intrepid explorers, Vikings discovered Iceland in the year 861 and, in fact, settled the country in 874. It is believed by some that America was first explored by Viking Chief Leif Ericson in the year 1000. If true, you can bet Ericson's ships had ale on board. Since the Vikings were almost always drunk, great amounts of ale were kept in huge casks on every vessel.

Viking brew was called "Aul." The Danes adapted Aul to "Ol" and from this came the English "ale." Of Viking ale, there were at least three kinds, all unhopped, slightly sweet, and potent. These ale types were clear ale, mild ale, and, the favorite, Welsh ale.

ALE AND THE VIKINGS

In Ireland during the 9th century, the Vikings are said to have brewed ale from heather using honey for fermentable sugar and adding wormwood as a bittering agent. Also, ales brewed with oats and bayberries were not uncommon.

Many drinking horns bore "ale runes" which were inscriptions to protect against deceitful women and poisons. Rune sticks covered with magical inscriptions were thrown into ale horncups to further defeat feminine wiles.

Ael (ale)-runes thou
must know, if thou wilt
not that another's wife
thy trust betray, if
thou in her confide. On
the horn must they be
graven.

Sigrdrifumal, The Lay of Sigrdrifa

ALE AND ETIQUETTE

When drinking horns were in short supply, the Vikings delighted in drinking ale from the boiled skulls of enemies killed in battle. While thus engaged in gory bliss, the warriors would often bleed themselves into each other's ale-skull in a brotherhood ceremony only death could undo. Such behavior notwithstanding, Vikings were the first known people to use tablecloths of pure white linen daily.

Blessing of your heart, you brew good Ale.

William Shakespeare,
<u>The Two Gentlemen of Verona</u>

Viking etiquette also called for getting one's enemies dead-drunk on ale and then burning down the ale-house with passed-out foes still inside.

ALE AND ETIQUETTE

Any pledge or statement made while drunk was legally binding and a Viking might awaken only to find that he was now someone's slave or had given away his wife or property.

To Norsemen, beer drunkenness was admirable and the measure of a man or woman was in one's ability to drink huge amounts of ale.

Dost thou think, because thou art virtuous, there shall be no more cakes and ale?

William Shakespeare, <u>Twelfth Night</u>

I will make it felony to drink small beer.

William Shakespeare, <u>King Henry VI</u>

Rents and taxes paid in beer and ale were called "ále-gafol" and ale tribute was exacted from all conquered tribes.

AN OCEAN OF ALE

Copious drinking was viewed by the Vikings in the same way that present-day people admire championship athletics.

When the god Thor was asked by the giant Utgard-Loki if Thor would care to compete in any feats of strength, Thor replied that he would rather compete in drinking. Utgard-Loki agreed, saying:

"From this (ale) horn it is thought to be well drunk if it is emptied in one draught, some men empty it in two, but there is no drinker so wretched that he cannot drain it in three." In spite of Thor's vast thirst, he was unable to drain Utgard-Loki's alehorn. The next day, however, Utgard-Loki confessed to Thor that the drinking contest was rigged. "Know then, that I have deceived you with illusions...When you drank from the horn, and thought so little ale was gone, it was a great wonder, which I thought not possible. One end of the horn stood in the sea, but that you did not see. When you come to the sea-shore you will discover how much the sea has sunk by your drinking. That is now the ebb of the tide."

In case you wonder what all this beer-drinking did to the Norseman's health and stamina...

I have never seen people with a more developed body stature than they. They are tall as date palms, blond and ruddy...They are the dirtiest creatures of God. They have no shame...Each one of them has from his nails to the neck figures of things tattooed in dark green.

Ibn Fadhlan, A.D. 922

Give me a woman who truly
loves beer, and I will
conquer the world.

Kaiser Wilhelm II (1859-1941)

Even though drunk on ale and beer, the Vikings were the absolute terror of the civilized world. Fearless, careless killers who ushered in the Dark Ages, the Norseman travelled in a state of ale-induced berserk! In this frenzied condition, the norsemen burned most of Europe to cinders. In return they gave the world the gift of ale. Looking back in time, maybe it wasn't such a bad deal.

And when I think upon a pot of beer.

Lord Byron (1788-1824), <u>Don Juan</u>

THE CHRONICLES OF
HEATHER ALE

In the history of Western Civilization, no beer has aroused so much speculation and curiosity as the 'lost' Heather ale of the Picts, small, dwarfish folk who were heavily tatooed (our word "picture" comes from "pict").

About the year 250 B.C., the Greek navigator and geographer Pytheas first explored and wrote of the land that we know as Scotland — and of the fierce, independent Picts. Living in villages deep underground, these tribal people were so ferocious that even the legions of Julius Caesar could not

subdue them. In the year 361 A.D., the
Emperor Julian witnessed the Picts in
battle and said the wild, ale-drunken
tribes sounded like "the bellowing of
oxen and the cawing of the raven."

Pict ale, the first beer brewed in
the British Isles, became famous for
its reported potency and hallucinogenic power.

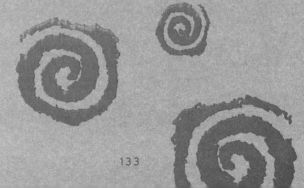

Doth it not show
vilely in me to
desire small beer?

William Shakespeare, <u>King Henry VI</u>

Incredible quantities of legyee (beer) were consumed, so as to raise the party to a degree of excitement necessary for a pro-longed revel.

Scheinfurth,
<u>Heart of Africa</u>, circa 1870

THE HEATHER BREW

The process of heather-ale brewing was a closely guarded secret of the Pict tribes (whose chieftains were sole keepers of the recipe), but it is known that Pict ale was made with the flowers and tops of specific heather plants whose blossoms were gathered, washed, and then placed in the bottom of brew vats. Wort, the liquid extract from malted grain, was then drained over the trough and the blooms to steep. Two parts heather to one part malt gave the resulting ale its supposed narcotic property. The specific variety of heather used was the basic secret in the brewing of this beer.

As late as the early 19th century, heather-ale brewing survived in small isolated areas of the Scottish Highlands. Sadly, the 'real stuff' died out sometime in the fourth century when Scottish King Niall led his forces to exterminate the Picts in Galloway.

Summer came in the country,
     Red was the heather bell;
But the manner of the brewing
     Was none alive to tell.
In graves that were like children's
     On many a mountain head,
The Brewsters of the Heather
     Lay numbered with the dead.

from <u>Heather Ale</u>
by Robert Louis Stevenson

It has been scientifi-
cally confirmed that
naturally occurring
ergot fungus containing
LSD-like properties
dwell beneath the leaves
of the heather plant.

In the realm of marriage, beer and
beer-drinking customs have survived
largely unchanged. The term bride
derives from the Germanic "bruths" and
the old English "bryd," both thought
to come from the root word "bru,"
meaning to brew or cook.

BEER AND MARRIAGE

At times, too much ale was brewed resulting in ale sales that continued for days after the wedding, all of which resulted in hoards of drunks lying about the scenery. Like night follows day, laws were passed.

...a payne is made that no person or persons that shall brewe any weddyn-ale to sell, shall not brewe above twelve strike of mault at the most, and that the said person so married shall not keepe or have above eight messe of persons at his dinner within the burrowe: and before his brydall daye he shall keep no unlawfull games in hys house, nor out of his house on pain of 20 shilling.

Court records, Hales-Owen Borough, Salpo County, England, circa 1598

When they come home from the church,
then beginneth excesse of eatying and
drinking and as much is wasted in one
days as were sufficient for the two
new-married folkes half a year to
lyve upon.

<u>In the Christian State of Matrimony</u>,
1543

In medieval times, it was customary for the parent of a betrothed couple to visit every house in the village, taking up a collection from the neighbors. The money was used to buy the ingredients to brew ale. Wedding ale required strength, and the belief was that weak or watered-down brew would result in an equally tepid marriage.

BEER IN THE KITCHEN

Be mine each morn with eager appetite
And hunger undissembled to repair
To friendly buttery; there on smoking
  crust
And foaming Ale to banquet unre-
  strained;
Material breakfeast! Thus in ancient
  days
Our ancesters robust with liberal cups
Usher'd the morn, unlike the squeamish
  sons
Of modern times.

                    Panegyric on Oxford Ale, 1748

Life, alas,
Is very drear.
Up with the
glass!
Down with the
beer!

Louis Untermeyer (1885-1977)

BEER AND THE BRIDE

In the middle ages "bride-ale" or "bridal," as it was known was at the wedding. Guests, friends, and relations would pay generously for each beer purchased. Strangers, travellers, and anyone not an invited wedding guest, would also pay a fixed price for each measure of brew. In so doing, the bride's dowery — the proceeds of the ale sales — would increase. At the end of the drunken festivities, a handsome nest-egg collected for the newly wed couple was given to the bride and groom.

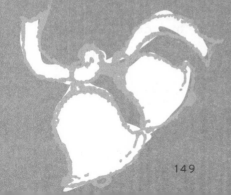

BEER AND THE WEDDING

In 1787, bridals had reached such
extremes that public invitations
were published in broadsides alert-
ing the public to ale for sale.

Suspend for one day your cares
and your labours,
And come to this wedding, kind
friends and good neighbours.
Notice is given that the marriage of
Isaac Pearson with Frances Atkinson
will be solemnized in due form in the
Parish Church of Lamplugh, Cumberland,
on Tuesday next, the 30th May after
which the bride and bridegroom, will
procede to Lonefoot, where the nup-
tials will be celebrated by a variety
of rural entertainments.

Public bridal invitation, 1787

Ere's to English
women an' a
quart of English
beer.

Rudyard Kipling

THE GROANING ALE

Lasting well into American colonial times, the custom of "groaning ales" marked the next phase of a wedded woman's career. When the time of a first child's birth was known, the local alewife or mother-in-law would brew a special high-test beer for "the time of the groaning" or childbirth. During labor, the mother-to-be and the midwives would swig from the ale pot to lend all extra strength for the ordeal.

FROM THE CRADLE

Records tell of washing
the newborn baby with
ale. The brew was known
to be pure and germ-free
– a real plus at a time
when water was suspect
for anything more than
washing your feet.

TO THE GRAVE

Here John Randal lies
Who counting of his tale
Lived threescore years and ten,
Such vertue was in his ale,
   Ale as his meat,
   Ale as his drink,
   Ale did his heart revive,
   And if he could have drunk his ale
   He still had been alive.
   He died January 5, 1699

Tombstone epitaph,
Great Walford, England

LEARN TO ENJOY IT

"Beer," he was shouting, "varies more than any other drink and is more of a gamble. You know that a bottle of a certain wine of a certain vintage should be drinkable, but you go into a strange pub and order a pint of four-ale you got no surety that it'll be any good. The pub-keeper may not take care of his pipes, his cellar may not be the right temperature. The beer may be sour or flat or one of a million other things. Beer, I tell you, is the hell of an undependable drink. In spite of the fact that he drinks it, an Englishman knows nothing about his national drink. So far as the Englishman is concerned, his beer might be a chemical compound that started its life in a laboratory at the other end of a pump, and it often tastes as if it was. The next time you take a glass of beer, my good fellow, think of it as a drink and not as medicine. Instead of ramming it back into your stomach — a disgustin' German students' trick — try tastin' it. Yes I said try tastin' it. Don't look so damned surprised. It won't poison you and you'll learn to enjoy it for its own sake."

Ruthven Todd (1914–1978)

Beer renders people stupid.

Otto Von Bismarck (1815-1898),
a prodigious beer-guzzler
and Head of State

THE CUSTOM OF DRINK

The moment a young German goes to the university of his choice, he puts on an absurd little cap, gets his face slashed, buys a boarhound, and devotes all his energies to drinking beer.

Mrs. Alfred Sidgwick,
Home Life in Germany, 1908

BEER AND THE GERMANS

Beer has been the life blood of the German people since the beginning of recorded history. The name "German" comes from the Celtic word "Germani" and means screamers or shouters — terms of endearment inspired by Germanic tribal battle cries.

"When they do not go to war, they spend much of their time at their leisure, doing nothing, only eating, drinking and sleeping...And it is notably the bravest warriors who do

nothing (but) lie prone on a bear
skin. As soon as they arise from
sleep,...late in the day, they
bathe...take their meal...then they
proceed to days and nights, without
intermission, in drinking. Their drink
is a liquor prepared from barley or
wheat brought by fermentation."

Tacitus, Roman historian, A.D. 98

Eighteen hundred years later, the German beer-drinker appears to be much the same!

The German begins drinking beer early in the morning. In place of coffee he takes beer which he stows away as a foundation on which to build the day's work — beer drinking. There are three things the Germans are intensely fond of: beer, music, and sauerkraut. And the principal occupation of the people — man, woman, and child — is beer drinking. German beer shops are on the corners of all the streets...beer shops are everywhere.

Henry Ruggles,
Germany Without Spectacles, 1883

A traveller to Munich for the Oktoberfest celebration, when asking directions to the beer tents, received the immortal words: "You can hear it two blocks away and smell it in three."

And what this flood of
deeper brown,
Which a white foam does
also crown,
Less white than snow,
more white than mortar?
Oh, my soul! Can this be
Porter?

The Dejeune

SAINTS, FESTIVALS,
AND FOOLS

Saint Monday. I still practice this holiday, which otherwise disappeared in the early 18th century. The idea was that any workman could take any Monday off as a holiday to drink beer in memory of a departed Saint, thus drinking deeply without penalty.

He who drinks beer sleeps well. **He who sleeps well cannot sin.** He who does not sin goes to heaven. **Amen.**

German Monk, name unknown

The clamorous crowd is
hushed with mugs of Mum
[German beer],Till all,
tuned equal, send a gen-
eral hum.

Alexander Pope (1688-1744)

When King William IV of Prussia visited Dortmund, Germany, a deputation of the magistrates waited upon him, one of them bearing a salver with a large tankard filled with "Adam" (10-year-old Dortmund strong ale). When the King asked what it was, and heard that it was the celebrated beer, he said, "Very welcome; for it is extremely warm," and drained off the tankard at a draught. His Majesty was unconscious for more than twenty-four hours.

Corvin, <u>An Autobiography</u>

GERMANY'S SAINTLY BEER DAYS

For the Germans who follow the saints there is Munich's Saint Joseph's Day held on March 19th and the spring fest called Fruhjahrsbierfest. South Munich has Saint Leonard's Day beer fest in November.

The best beer
is where the
priests go to
drink.

Anonymous, 16th century

The saloon is a very spiritual place. "Ah, God love ya," my white-haired Irish bartender says to me, pocketing my lavish tip while, down the rail, a drinker mutters, "Jesus! This beer is wretched!" A mere hour before, another patron announced, "God, this is great stuff!," dipping his mug into his mug of amber brew.

They sell good beer at Haslemere
And under Guildford Hill.
At little Cowfold as I've been told
A beggar may drink his fill:
There is a good brew in Amberley too,
And by the bridge also;
But the swipes they take in at the
Washington Inn
Is the very best Beer I know.

Hilaire Belloc (1870-1953)

It is better to think of church in the ale-house than to think of the ale-house in church.

Martin Luther (1483-1546)

During the Middle Ages, nearly every abbey brewed beer for the faithful flock within the walls. Beer was critical to good diet. But soon, the church weaseled into the business of beer, selling to the unwashed masses outside. As a logo, the abbeys used each other's patron saint to create brand recognition, even if that particular saint never touched a drop.

The selling of
bad beer **is a**
crime against
Christian love.

Law, the City of Augsburg,
13th century

SAINTLY SUDS

Saints abound on scores of beers such as St. Austell's, Saint Edmund's Ale, the non-alcoholic Saint Christopher, Saint Neots Bitter, Bishop's Tipple, and Bishop's Finger — the latter hopefully extended in blessing. Wales offers Saint David's Porter, and Scotland has Saint James Scottish Ale, France produces Saint Landelin, Saint Amant, Saint Léonard and Saint Hildegarde. Belgium, as all lovers of fine beer know, is perhaps best known for sanctified beer brands with Saint Sixtus, Saint Bernardus Pater, Saint Benoit, Saint Hubert, Saint Idesbald, Saint Louis, Saint

Amands, Saint Feuillion, and Saint
Christoffel. Saint Norbert oversees
the brewing of Grimbergen beers.
Germany offers Saint Jacobus Bock,
Saint Josef's, and Saint Thomas Brau
of Nussdorf.

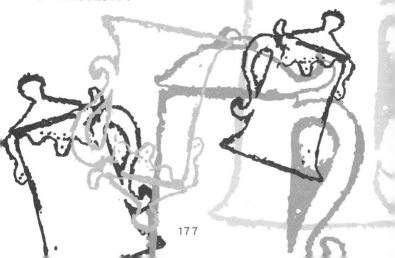

SAINTS, FESTIVALS, AND FOOLS

Feast of Fools. Another quaint medieval custom, the Fools' Feast was held inside the church on the Feast of Saint Stephen, December 26, and the Feasts of Saint John (December 27) and the Holy Innocents (December 28). A mock priest would conduct a mass while the ale-drunken crowd in the pews would bray back obscene responses. After the "mass," the ale-drunken revellers would sing and dance their way through the streets.

I cannot eat but
little meat,
  My stomach is not
good;
But sure I think
that I can drink
  With him that wears
a hood.

Anonymous

Many pubs bear the name Saint Crispin. While I cannot determine if Crispin was fond of the odd pint or not, he was patron saint of shoemakers and cobblers. Crispin, beheaded in A.D. 308, made shoes for the poor, resulting in his death and the old homily "cobblers and tinkers make the best ale drinkers." Saint Julian, once patron saint of travellers, was a natural for an inn sign. Saint Julian's logo was three crosses.

There hang three crosses at
   thy door,
Hang up thy wife and she'll
   make four.

Dean Swift,
comment to a tavern keeper

Saint John The Baptist's head...Good Eating

Pub sign, as noted by William Hogarth (1697-1764), English painter

SAINTS, FESTIVALS, AND FOOLS

Saint Paul's Eve. This was a Welsh beer fest for the wretched tin miners. After work, miners would throw stones at a pitcher full of beer until the jug is hit and broken. Then they would drink.

BEER AND THE POET

"Drink water," cried William; had
    all men done so,
You'd never have wanted a coach-
    man, I trow.
They are soakers, like me, whom
    you load with reproaches,
That enable you brewers to ride
    in your coaches.

       17th century English poem

It is my design to die in the brew-house; let ale be placed to my mouth when I am expiring, that when the choirs of angels come, they may say, "Be God propitious to this drinker."

Saint Columbanus, A.D. 612

BEER

One of the first full-fledged saints of beer was Saint Columbanus, who was sent to convert the fallen to Christ. Stumbling upon a group of heathen about to sacrifice a vat of ale to the god Wodan, the fledgling Saint hollered, "Stop!" and blew on the ale cask from across the clearing. With an awful explosion, the cask blew into pieces. Explaining to the frightened pagans that good ale was wasted on the devil, Columbanus asked if any more brew was around. The unbaptized replied "yes," and more ale appeared from its hiding place. Columbanus explained that ale was the beloved of God but only when drunk in His Holy Name.

Saintly women numbered among those who liked beer, including Saint Brigid of Ireland, the abbess of Kildare (A.D. 439-521). One hot day, while working in a colony of lepers, she found her patients to be exceedingly thirsty after their bath. To answer their pleas, with Christ's blessing she changed the bathwater into beer.

For when the lepers she
nursed implored her for
beer and there was none to
be had, she changed the
water which was used for
the bath into an excellent
beer, by the sheer strength
of her blessing, and dealt
it out to the thirsty in
plenty.

Vita Sanctae Brigidae
(Life of St. Brigid)

Saint Hildegard, the abbess
of Diessenberg, was an
herbalist whose writings
include the earliest-known
references to the application
of hops in brewing beer.

(Hops), when put in beer,
stops putrification and
lends longer durability.

Saint Hildegard (A.D. 1098-1179)
Benedictine nun

If but we
Christians
have our beer,
nothing's to
fear.

Sir William Ashbless

A HOLY BREW

While moving the bones of Saint Arnoldus from the churchyard to the church workmen struggled with carrying the heavy casket up a steep hill on a very hot day. Someone muttered in the heat, "Jesus, I wish I had a cool beer." At that moment, streams of cold ale shot out of the casket drenching those below. All had lots of drink and a new saint was discovered.

The French Bishop of Metz,
also known as Saint
Arnoldus, spent his holy
life warning the peasants
about the dangers of drinking water.
From man's sweat and God's
love, beer came into the
world.

Saint Arnoldus

God made yeast, as well as
dough, and loves fermentation just as dearly as he
loves vegetation.

Ralph Waldo Emerson (1803-1882)

BEER LORD'S PRAYER

Our barrel which is on draught
let your beer tap, its will be done.
Be in all the restaurants and pubs,
and forgive our thirst
as we forgive our waiters,
and lead us not to the police
station, but deprive us of
all the nasty teetotallers.

> Found on workers' toilet wall,
> brewery in Slovakia

Tribes do their most heroic beer drinking in good times, not bad, and anxiety plays no part in beer orgies. Charcoal from the campfire goes into the fermenting jar; they say, to keep the spirits of the dead away from the brew.

SAINTS, FESTIVALS, AND FOOLS

Tap-Up Sunday. The Sunday before the 2nd of October was a 'holy' day on which anyone and everyone could (and did) sell beer without a license. Peculiar to Guilford, England, this day was held in tribute to God's gifts: beer and barley.

BEER AND SONG

And now my song has come to an end.
My homeward way I soon must wend.
I'm hoping that the gods will send
Another round of porter.

Traditional Irish song

Beer is indeed divine stuff. So, next time at the bar, buy a stranger the Poculum Charitatis — the loving cup of ale.

A LITERARY BREW

When I die I want to decompose in a barrel of porter and have it served in all the pubs in Dublin. I wonder, would they know it was me?

J.P. Donleavy, _The Ginger Man_, 1955

BEER ON THE AMAZON

Ten millennium ago, in the Amazon
Rain Forests, complex, planned farms
grew corn and manioc — the two main
staples for chicha (corn) and masato
(manioc) beers.

Chaco tribes drank too much beer, believing a drunken person dreams of beautiful things. Men sang and drummed through the night to hasten the fermentation of the beer and the rites of beer-making were as important as the beer itself.

According to
ancient
Amazonian legend
young, pretty
virgins are
believed to make
the best brew.

Peruvian Quechua Indians drink chicha from quart glasses, a custom that continues today.

DRINKING WITH THE DEAD

A step in the process of embalming was the "Liturgy of Opening the Mouth," a ceremony that took place after the mummification rites but before final entombment. The body was unwrapped and beer was poured into the mouth of the corpse — a last gargle into the great beyond.

Man's way to god is with beer in the hand.

Koffyar tribe saying

BEER AND BURIAL

For the Koffyar people of Nigeria the ritual sharing of beer between the living and the dead has continued for thousands of years. On their tombs sit glasses with no bottom, set into an earthen mound. The glasses receive offerings of beer that quickly spread into a dark stain on the dry dust of the grave.

YOU CAN TAKE IT WITH YOU

For the Egyptians, much of this life was spent preparing for the next life. The affluent dead took entire miniature breweries, complete with tiny wooden brewers, into the darkness of the grave.

Wine made from barley...was very strong, and of delicious flavor...but the taste must be acquired.

Xenophon, 400 B.C.

Rare beers like "The Beer of Truth," were placed alongside the dead to tempt the twelve gods who would sit in judgment of the deceased. The hope was to intoxicate the gods into a kinder assessment of the soul in purgatory.

BEER OF THE DEAD

Other Egyptian funerary beers were "Everlasting Beer" and "The Beer Which Does Not Sour" — both guaranteed to put the sternest of gods into a mood of forgiveness.

When a dead body
was laid in the
grave, his beer
(the priest's
payment) was
seven jars.

The last King of Lagash,
ancient Assyria

When the hour
is nigh me,
Let me in a
tavern die,
With a tankard
by me.

Archpoet, Confessio, 12th century

FOOD AND DRINK

Among the forest tribes of Latin America, eating the dead enemy was called "exocannibalism," while eating the bodies of one's own relations was called "endocannibalism." Legend has it that you couldn't beat the taste of human fingers with a cool skull cup of chicha beer.

The pleasure of beer is still savored by those in the spirit world and the dead demand their share of suds. Tapajos, Cubeos, Arapium, and Panoans all mixed the bones of their relatives into special brews.

Other groups cremated the corpses, then added the ashes into beer. Still others painted the bones before powdering the remains. For the brewsters, bone ash acted as finings or clarifiers in beer, drawing particulate matter out of the brew, making the beer clearer. But the logic of beer of the dead was to keep the spirits of the dead within the living tribe.

The Putumayo River tribes ate captives only after an eight-day beer festival where the prisoners, soon to be dinner, were kept drunk until meal time.

BEER AND BURIAL

Jivaro women were buried with their brew pots and beer strainers all scattered around their heads. Following burial, and for at least a year after, fresh beer was placed on top of the burial mound for benefit of the spirit of the deceased.

217

Under the Cathedral church at Hereford
is the greatest Charnel-house for
bones that I ever saw in England. In
A.D. 1650 there lived amongst those
bones a poor old woman that, to help
out her fire (income), did use to mix
the deadmen's bones; this was thrift
and poverty: but cunning alewives put
the ashes of these bones in their ale
to make it intoxicating.

John Aubrey (1626-1697), Brief Lives

A VIKING BURIAL

When a Viking of rank was buried, his entire household — lesser ranked wives, slave girls, goats, pigs, chickens and favorite battle ax and all — went with him. Plied with lots of ale before having their throats slit prior to being tossed more alive than dead onto the funeral pyre, these victims of sacrifice would go with the dead to serve him in death just as they had in life.

For the Norsemen, heaven (Valhalla) was a vast ale-house of divine pro-portions, with 540 doors. Inside, dead Vikings drank from lim-itless streams of ale that sprang from the udders of the giant goat Heidrun.

A NATIONAL PASTIME

In my innocence I once
thought that beer drinking
in England was carried to
excess, but I was mistaken.
Englishmen are in the
infant class — in the AC's
— in acquiring a German's
education in the practice
of beer drinking.

Henry Ruggles, 1883

CHURCHYARD BEER-DRINKING

In England and the British Isles those about to meet their maker left testaments in their wills, providing for ale to be brewed and given away on the date of their death.

Thou reprobate mortal!
Why, dost thou not know
Whither, after your death,
all you drunkards must go?
Must go when we're dead?
Why, sir, you may swear,
We shall go, one and all,
where we find the best
beer.

An anonymous minister, circa 1880

And give a hand
to an old man
filled with
beer.

The Instruction of Amenemope,
11th century B.C.

In rural Norway, tradition held that the ale itself had a spirit. Silence ruled the brew-house. "Don't startle the ale!" the brewster would say, putting a piece of iron in the brew kettle to keep the evil dead away from the beer.

A LITERARY BREW

But to her, death was the
end of everything. At one
with the One, it didn't
mean a thing beside a glass
of Guinness on a sunny day.

Graham Greene, <u>Brighton Rock</u>, 1938

Beer has drowned more than the sea.

Pablius Syrus

DROWNING IN BEER

I n London, England, on the 16th of October, 1814, at the brewery of Meux and Company, a 22-foot-high vat of strong ale holding the equivalent of 4,000 casks of beer lay quietly maturing in the brewhouse. The vessel was held together with 29 giant iron hoops. On that fateful day, a workman noticed one hoop on the brew vat had a small crack and an hour later, disaster struck. With a boom heard five miles away, the huge vat exploded. A tremendous jet stream of ale shot out, crushing a smaller vessel holding an additional 2,400 barrels of brew, creating a tidal wave, that smashed down the 25-foot-high, one-foot-thick brick wall of the brewery.

Eyewitnesses told of besotted mobs flinging themselves into gutters full of beer, hampering rescue efforts. Many were killed, suffocated in the crush of hundreds trying to get to a free beer.

For weeks following the great flood of beer, the entire region was rank with the odor of stale ale, despite the efforts of local fire brigades to pump out streets and cellars. The death toll eventually reached 20, including some deaths from alcohol coma. An inquest was held to determine if anyone was liable for the catastrophe. The jury's verdict: Death by casualty.

The English working classes may be said to be soaked in beer. They are made dull and sodden by it. Children are...born to the smell and taste of it, and brought up in the midst of it.

Jack London, 1903

If the home we never write to, and
  the oaths we never keep,
  and all we know most distant and
  most dear,
Across the snoring barrack-room return
  to break our sleep,
  can you blame us if we soak
  ourselves in beer?

Rudyard Kipling

Where you and I
went down the
lane with ale
mugs in our
hands...

G.K. Chesterton (1874-1936)

A LITERARY BREW

"Did you ever taste beer?" "I had a sip of it once," said the small servant. "Here's a state of things!" cried Mr. Swiveller...."She never tasted it—it can't be tasted in a sip!"

> Charles Dickens (1812-1870),
> Nicholas Nickleby

I wish I was a brewer's
  horse
**For twelve months in the
  year,**
I'd put my head where my
  tail should be
And suck up all the beer.

Thomas Randall, 1642

BEER AND SONG

At noon, the haymakers sit them down,
To drink from their bottles of ale
  nut-brown;
In summer too, when the weather is warm,
A good bottle full will do them no harm.
The lads and the lasses begin to tattle
But what would they do without this
  bottle.
There's never a lord, an earl or knight,
But in this bottle doth take delight;
For when he's hunting of the deer,
He oft doth wish for a bottle of beer.
Likewise the man that works in the wood,
A bottle of beer will oft do him good.

The Roxburghe Ballads, circa 1560

The ancient Egyptians authored hundreds of hymns to Hathor, the goddess of drunkenness and the inventress of beer.

BEER AND SONG

I kiss her
Her lips open
And I am drunk
Without a beer.

Song of the Harper, found in chapel
of King Inyotef, ancient Egypt

JOHN TAYLOR —
THE BARD OF BEER

John Taylor, born in Gloucester, England on August 24, 1580 was the self-styled poet laureate of beer and ale. An adventurer, saloon keeper, publisher and, for forty years, the greatest advocate of good beer and ale that ever lived, Taylor extolled the virtues of a pot of good ale in more than 100 tracts and pamphlets.

Following a stint in the Royal Navy, John Taylor began a series of eccentric journeys around England for which he solicited subscribers to support his adventures. Taylor believed that the best beer equaled the best lodging. If no inn or pub were to be had, Taylor presented himself at the front door of the local big-wig in town asking for lodging for the night. Representing himself as "the Queen's Waterman" and "the King's Water-poet," Taylor immortalized his hosts in return for cakes and ale.

John Taylor's success in this gambit was nothing less than astounding. He appears to have been welcomed everywhere and, true to his word, returned kindness with glowing written tributes to his many hosts on the quality of their ale. Taylor's writings became so well known that free food and beer were literally thrust upon the traveller wherever he went.

The waiter's hands that
  reach
To each his perfect pint of
  stout
His proper chop to each.

Alfred, Lord Tennyson (1809-1892)

BEER AND EDUCATION

Life isn't all beer and skittles; but beer and skittles, or something better of the same sort, must form a good part of every Englishman's education.

Thomas Hughes,
<u>Tom Brown's Schooldays</u>, 1857

JOHN TAYLOR'S
BARROOM BET

The poet John Taylor was a relentless bettor. One day in a pub, Taylor made a bet that he could sail in a boat made entirely of paper from London to Queenborough, nearly 50 miles. Perhaps under the influence of his beloved ale when this bizarre bet was made, nonetheless, Taylor launched his strange craft, built only of oiled paper, onto the Thames. While crowds of cheering rabble followed along the riverbank, Taylor rowed out. He made it — wet, but undaunted — all the way to Queensborough to collect his money.

Beer that is
not drunk had
missed its
vocation.

Meyer Breslau, 1880

A DRINKER'S MAP

Shortly before his death, John Taylor penned the first beer guide for connoisseurs. His book was a catalog of the best inns and taverns to be found in all ten shires around London with special emphasis placed on the quality of each tavern's ale. During his life, Taylor owned two saloons — one in Oxford and a second in Covent Garden. He died while serving pints at the latter, The Poets Head Inn, in December 1653.

Then high and mighty town's ale I did
    drink there.
It made my brains to caper and
    career,
It was of such magnificent strong
    force,
To knock me in five miles twice from
    my horse.

                              John Taylor

A LITERARY BREW

Beer, of course, is actually a
depressant, but poor people will never
stop hoping otherwise.

Kurt Vonnegut, Jr., <u>Hocus Pocus</u>, 1990

Keep your libraries, keep your penal institutions, keep your insane asylums...give me beer. You think man needs rule, he needs beer. The world does not need your morals it needs beer. It does not need your lectures or your charity. The souls of men have been fed with indigestibles, but the soul could make use of beer.

Henry Miller (1891-1980)

Beer songs have even found their way into grand opera. The Italian opera Marta, first performed in 1847, contained the Canzone del Porter — The Porter Song.

A LYRIC BREW

You foam within our glasses, you
  lusty golden brew,
Whoever imbibes takes fire from you.
The young and old sing your praises,
Here's to beer, here's to cheer,
  here's to beer.

Lyrics from the opera "The Bartered
Bride," by Smetana, 1866

On the chest of a barmaid
  in Sale
Were tattooed the prices of
  ale.
And on her behind
For the sake of the blind
Was the same information in
  Braille.

Anonymous

BEER ETIQUETTE

Catastrophic-doom expectation syndrome: The fear of showing up at a gathering with the wrong brew — which is fast becoming America's most dreaded social faux pas.

What's made
Milwaukee
famous, made a
loser out of
me...

Jerry Lee Lewis

The rolling English
drunkard made the rolling
English road.

G.K. Chesterton (1874-1936)

BEER AND THE BLUES

My honey came in; she blew her top, Lord I thought she'd never stop. Well, she's my honey and I love her dear, but she don't want me to drink beer. If you love me you'll understand, I want beer. I'm a beer drinkin' man.

"Beer Drinkin' Blues" by Crowe/Pyle, circa, 1940, sung by Rocky Bellford

I'm seein' the road that I traveled,
  a road paved with heartaches and
  tears,
I'm seein' the past that I've wasted,
  while watchin' the bubbles in my
  beer.
I think of the heart that I've broken
  and of the golden chances that have
  past me by...
The dreams I once made are now empty,
  as empty as the bubbles in my beer.

> "Bubbles in My Beer"
> Walker/Duncan/Wills, circa 1940,
> Sung by Bob Wills

My two large pigs,
by drinking some beer
grounds...got so amazingly
drunk by it, they were not
able to stand and appeared
like dead things almost...I
never saw pigs so drunk in
my life.

James Woodford,
Diary of a Country Parson, 1758-1802

A LITERARY BREW

This miller hath so
wisely bibbed ale,
That as an hors he
snorteth in his slepe.

Chaucer, <u>Canterbury Tales</u>

Beer is a light, narcotic, alcoholic beverage, which charms us into a state of gladness and soft hilarity; it protects our hearts against stings of all kinds, awaiting us in this valley of misery; it diminishes the sensitiveness of our skin to the nettles and to all the bites of the numberless, detestable human insects that hum, hiss, and hop about us. The happy mortal who has selected beer as his preferred stimulant imbeds greater griefs and joys in soft pillows; surely thus being wrapped up he will be able to travel through this stormy life with less danger.

BEER ETIQUETTE

At social parties no gen-
tleman ever thought of
leaving the table sober;
the host would have considered it a slight on his
hospitality.

F.W. Hackwood, comment on manners,
18th century England

If you couldn't
afford good
whiskey, he'd
take you on
trust for beer.

Gerald Brennan, Floriut, Shanahan's
Ould Shebeen, 1899

BEER NOIR

Understand he's been having
a little beer. Well won't
hurt him any. Won't do him
any good, but there's
damned little that will.
Not enough alcohol in the
slop they make these days
to hurt a baby.

Jim Thompson, A Swell-Looking Babe,
1954

THE DANGERS OF DRINK

I am told that you neglect your studies, have a desire for enjoyments, and go from tavern to tavern. Whoever smells of beer is repulsive to all; the smell of beer holds people at a distance, it hardens your soul...You think it proper to run down a wall and to break through the board gate; the people run away from you. You beat them until sore...Do not give the mugs a place in your heart; forget the goblets;...You sit in the hall, you are surrounded by the nymphs; you arise and act foolishly...you sit in front of the girl, you are rubbed with oil, a wreath of

burrs is around your neck; you bet
your stomach like a drum, you stum-
ble, you fall upon your stomach, you
are smeared with filth.

Papyrus Sallier I and Papyrus Anastasi
                    IV, ancient Egypt

A POET'S PINT

Fill with mingled cream and amber
  I will drain that glass again.
Such hilarious visions clamber
  Through the chamber of my brain —
Quaintest thoughts — queerest fancies
  Come to life and fade away:
What care I how time advances?
  I am drinking ale today.

Edgar Allan Poe (1809-49)

Beer... "a high and mighty liquor"

Julius Caesar

Pay-day came, and with it beer.

Rudyard Kipling

BEER'S BEGINNINGS

In hidden, remote places around the world from the jungles of South America to the steppes of Asia, women still hold close the arts of brewing. Praying to their ancient goddesses, the women of non-technological societies continue to pass down to their daughters the secrets of beer. The old ways have not gone but soon will be.

At eve the day is to be
praised; a woman after she
is burnt; a sword after it
is proved; a maid after she
is married; ice after it
has passed away; beer after
it is drunk.

The Viking Edda, 11th century

I lived from bread of black wheat, **and drank from beer of white wheat.**

Ancient Egyptian funeral inscription, as cited in Coffin Tests III, by A. DeBuck

DEPRIVED OF DRINK

Nothing in the whole animal kingdom is viler than a brewer when he is robbed of his drink. The war measures [temperance] have touched the pocketbooks of the brewers, and they are now furious. They are foaming with rage.

Mr. Larsen-Ledet, 1920

A DEMOCRATIC BREW

Beer goes with the crowd to Coney Island, lodge picnics and clam bakes. It follows the races, attends prize fights and ball games. It accompanies the fisherman to the brook and awaits him in the coolness of the spring. It rides the Twentieth Century, lives at the Ritz, and greets the dusty traveller at the hot dog stand. The furtive maid opens it on the kitchen table for her sweetheart while the butler serves it to his master on a silver tray. It christens the freshman, returns the alumnus and presides at the midnight feast.

Obie Winters

A long experience with
clients has made me prefer
a shabby whisky-drinker to
a well-dressed beer-drinker.

Graham Greene (1904-1991)

[Beer] is an
excellent wash.

Goode Queene Bess

In the grand scheme of things, the doctors and healers of the last 5,000 years seem to have respected beer as a positive component in the lives of patients.

The greatest medical text of ancient times — The Papyrus Eber — gave ancient Egyptians nearly 600 prescriptions for the entire catalog of human suffering. More than 100 of these cures listed beer as the principal ingredient.

His earthly abode [body]
was torn and broken by
beer. His Ka [spirit]
escaped before **it was
called by God.**

Egyptian medical writing,
circa 2800 B.C., first known
description of death by alcoholism

A tasty remedy against
death wilt thou take hath
an onion stepped in stef
[beer foam].

Papyrus Ebers

BEER AND SONG

March Beer is a drink for a King,
Then let us be merry, wash sorrow
  away,
Beer and ale shall be drunk to-day.

       17th century English song

An ancient Greek complaint was that beer drinking caused the drinker to urinate far too often than was decent for the refined Grecian way of life.

THE DANGERS
OF DRINKING BEER

Attention has been called to the large number of bartenders who have lost fingers on both hands...an employee of (a saloon) lost three fingers from his right hand, two from his left, and the physicians decided that they became rotted off by the beer which he handled.

AMA Quarterly, 1889

BEER IS GOOD FOR YOU,
BEER IS BAD FOR YOU

Surgeon Brown...contended that bad
water and sewerage in Belfast had
caused typhoid and typhus fever in
that town. Mr. Mowatt replied that
those who had suffered most from
fever drank "Bass's bitter ale" and
"Guinness' stout" and not Belfast
water.

Transactions of Social Science
Congress, 1867

Beer was not
made to be
moralized about,
but to be
drunk.

Theodore Maynard

AN ACQUIRED TASTE

A brewer, who, when asked by the Doctors, "Do you know what filthy water they use in brewing?" replied, "Oh yes, I know all about it, and the more filthy the water the better. In the brewery in which I work, the pipes which draw the water from the river come in just at the place which receive the drainings from the horse stables; and there is no better beer in the world as is made from it.

AMA Journal, 1837

A LITERARY BREW

It was the most beautiful colour that the eye of an artist in beer could desire; full in body, yet brisk as a volcano; piquant, yet without a twang; luminous as an autumn sunset; free from streakiness of taste; but, finally, rather heady. The masses worshipped it, the minor gentry loved it more than wine, and by the most illustrious country families it was not despised.

Thomas Hardy, _The Trumpet-Major_

If you carry out a blind-
fold test...you'll find
that the beer snob is just
as much a galah as the wine
snob.

Cyril Peark,
<u>Beer, Glorious Beer</u>, 1969

BEER IS GOOD FOR YOU, BEER IS BAD FOR YOU

Malt liquors may be considered wholesome, if used in moderation, by lean, nervous, cold, bloodless persons, but not by individuals of full habit.

E.B. Foote, M.D., 1902

In appearance, the beer-drinker may be the picture of health, but in reality he is most incapable of resisting disease.

Quarterly Journal of Inebriety, 1850

THE DANGERS OF DRINK

The increasing use of beer is worse than all the plagues of Egypt...This sodden, drooling, half-witted style of drunkenness which substitutes a stupid, boozy mass for the old-fashioned few (hard liquor drinkers), wide-awake with delirium tremens, a disease which was characterized by a certain fatal liveliness and dispatch far preferable to the wheezy and idiotic stupors of the beer guzzlers.

M.W. Blair, 1888

Beer is the drunkard's kindergarten.

Garrison Keillor

There are **more** old drunks than old doctors.

Anonymous

THE DANGERS
OF DRINKING OUTSIDE

The beer garden recently started on this side of the river, continues to grow offensive. The rabble from the city and the country meet there and sometimes form nothing less than drunken mobs. It is not safe for women to pass along the road near this place. Bloody fights are of a daily occurrence and drunken men may be found lying around in the bushes on all sides. Wife whipping has come into vogue since the new institution was forced upon us....

Badger State Banner, 1890, as quoted by Michael Lesy, _Wisconsin Death Trip_

We don't know why beer-drink-ing rodents developed fewer tumors. Follow-up studies must be done.

Dr. Richard Nelson,
University of Illinois, 1986

A BEERY RECOVERY

About 1730, the Earl of Bath, lay sick, of a pleuritic feaver... He was still alive, and was heard to mutter, in a low voice, "Small beer, small beer!" Accordingly a great silver cup was brought, which held two quarts of small beer. Pulteney drank off the whole at a draught, and demanded another. Another cupful was administered to him, and soon after that he fell into a profuse perspiration and a profound slumber. From that time forth he recorded wonderfully, insomuch that in a few days the physicians took leave of him.

John Timbs, 16th century

COLONIAL LIFE

A 1854 dispatch from the colony in New South Wales reads, "Of Doctors and medicines we have in plenty more than enough . . . what you may, for the Love of God, send is some large quantity of beer."

They who drink
beer will think
beer.

Washington Irving and
William Warburton

THE REMEDIAL BREW

Ale is a singular remedy against all melancholic diseases, tremor cordis, and maladies of the spleen; it is purgative and of great operation against iliaca passic, and all grippings of the small guts; it cures the stone in the bladder and kidneys and provokes urine wonderfully; it mollifies tumors and swellings in the body; and is very predominant in opening obstructions of the liver. Ale is most effectual for clearing the sight, being applied outwardly it asswageth the insufferable pain of gout, the yeast being laid hot to the part pained. It is easeful to pain in the

hip called sciatica; indeed, for all
defluxions and epidemic diseases what-
soever, and equal good against all
contagious diseases, feavers, agues,
rhumes, choughes, and all cattarres —
of all sicknesses — ale doth heal.

John Taylor (1580-1653),
The Bard of Beer

BEER ETIQUETTE

Fermentaphobia: A syndrome of paralyzing, often crippling fear experienced when faced with the numbing task of having to choose a particular beer for a social gathering from dozens of selections.

"Come, my lad,
and drink some
beer."

Samuel Johnson (1709-1784)

BEER REMEDIES

Hot beer is excellent good for the keeping of the stomach in good order...so it is most excellent for the quenching of thirst. For I have not known thirst since I have used hot beer; let the weather be never so hot, and my work great, yet have I not felt thirst as formerly...Cold beer is very pleasant when extreme thirst is in the stomach; but what more dangerous to the health. Many by drinking a cup of cold beer in extreme thirst, have taken a surfeit and killed themselves. Therefore we must not drink cold beer...

Henry Overton, 1641

A can of beer'd
be the makin'
of a guy a cold
mornin' like
this.

John Dos Passos (1896-1970)

BEER ETIQUETTE

If taking lunch at Claridges, you were to call loudly for a tankard of old ale, you would lay yourself open to three imputations. First...that you had no appreciation of good food; second that you failed to be suitably impressed by your surroundings; and third and worst and most unexpected of all, that you were addicted to genteelisms. And every one of these imputations would be unjust. With certain dishes...there is no drink superior to, more congenial and appropriate than, old ale.

Anonymous, 1934

I **have fed purely** upon ale;
I have ate my ale, and I
always sleep upon ale.

> George Farquhar (1678-1707),
> The Beaux' Stratagem

A DEMOCRATIC BREW

I think if I had to say one thing about beer, above all others, it's that beer is a democracy. From the very earliest beginnings of human settlements and civilization, beer halls were the levelers of classes. When you walked through those swinging doors in Sumer or Babylon, you were on democratic common ground. This was the value of the tavern or the public house or beer garden—what a wonderful notion!

Beer is the cause of all the radical pot-politics that men talk over it.

Otto Van Bismark (1815-1898)

The Puritanical nonsense of
excluding children and —
therefore — to some extent
women from pubs has turned
these places into mere
boozing shops instead of
the family gathering places
that they ought to be.

George Orwell (1903-1950)

BEER ETIQUETTE

And there are few things in this life so revolting as sipped beer. But let it go down your throat "as suds go down the drain," and you will quickly realize that this is a true friend, to be admitted to your most secret counsels. Long draughts with an open throat are the secret.

Maurice Healy, 1940

BEER BORES

I pour a round of Lowenbrau, being careful not to pour along the side but straight down so the beer can express itself, and they say, "Did you ever try Dockendorf?" It's made by the Dockendorf family from hand-pumped water in their ancient original family brewery in an unspoiled Pennsylvania village where the barley is hauled in by Amish families who use wagons with oak beds. Those oak beds give Dockendorf its famous flavor. These beer bores...

Garrison Keillor,
<u>Lake Wobegon Days</u>, 1985

Listening to someone
who brews his own
beer is like listen-
ing to a religious
fanatic talk about
the day he saw the
light.

Ross Murray, Montreal Gazette, 1991

THE CRITIC

When I conducted a beer-rating session last year, I wrote that most American beers taste as if they were brewed through a horse. This offended many people in the American beer industry, as well as patriots who thought I was being subversive in praising foreign beers. Now I must apologize. I have just read a little-known study of American beers. So I must apologize to the horse. At least with a horse, we'd know what we're getting.

Mike Royko (1932-1997)

Beer makes you feel **the way you** ought to feel without beer.

Henry Lawson

AND FOR DINNER...

Fill a large casserole with good baking apples, sugar, and lemon. Seal with a roll of rich pastry crust, and bake. When done, remove crust, divide into triangular pieces, and arrange around the apples in the casserole. Pour over all 1 quart hissing hot ale. Serve with spit-roasted ox, blackbird pie, or roasted boar.

William Hone,
Every-Day Book, 1826-7

For it (beer) possesses the essential quality of gulpability. Beer is more gulpable than any other beverage and consequently it ministers to the desire to drink deeply. When one is really thirsty the nibbling, quibbling, sniffing, squinting technique of the winner connoisseur becomes merely idiotic. Then is the moment of the pint tankard of bitter.

Anonymous, 1934

I think this
would be a good
time for a
beer.

Franklin D. Roosevelt, 1933

A FINAL BREW

Mary Queen of Scots, who was partial to the brown beer of Burton-on-Trent, and had supplies of this excellent brew sent to her during her long captivity at Fotheringay. It helped her to pass the days until her execution in 1587. Sir Walter Raleigh, on the morning of his execution in 1618, treated himself to a cool tankard and a soothing pipe of tobacco.

John Watney, 1974

TEMPERANCE & PROHIBITION

The American Temperance Movement was never concerned with temperate enjoyment of beer and other alcoholic beverages. An oxymoron, Temperance was a term meaning the total eradication of all alcoholic drinks and the places that served them — especially the "Devil's playground," the Saloon.

Women were thought exempt from temptations of the bar-room. It would take Prohibition in the 1920s to introduce millions of females to the pleasures of saloons and cocktails in the home.

TEMPERANCE

Friday night saloons were invaded by scores of women — all dressed in their Sunday best — singing at the top of their lungs such old evergreens as "Nearer My God To Thee," "Lips That Touch Liquor Shall Never Touch Mine," or "Has My Darling Willy Been Here Tonight?" Such caterwauling drove all but the most hardened beer drinkers out into the night. As women were responsible for creating these disturbances — respectable women at that — police were loath to interfere by arresting the ladies for breach of peace.

THE FIRST DROP

The use of beer is especially damaging to boys...these stimulants excite the passions, and produce a clamoring for sensual gratification which few boys or young men have the will-power or moral courage to resist.

J.H. Kellogg, M.D., 1888

Everyone hath a penny for the new Alehouse.

Thomas Fuller, 1732

At the Fifteenth International Congress Against Alcoholism, **held in Washington, D.C., in 1920, Dr. Stockard of Cornell University and Dr. C.W. Saleeby of London recommended the establishment of concentration camps for chronic beer drinkers.**

THE DANGERS OF DRINK

Three quarts a day is an average amount for a "true Bavarian" while thousands...accommodate eight quarts a day the year round. Though there is little of what is politely called "drunkenness" among them, the habit of beer drinking causes want, idleness, disease, squalor, vice, and crime to abound. As an outcome of this habit, a great proportion of the people are too poor to marry...and hence, fully one-half of their children are of illegitimate birth — a scandal to all pretension to civilization.

Elisah Chenery, M.D., 1889

Is the wisdom in the can?

Old Dutch saying

I would give
all my fame for
a pot of ale,
and safety.

William Shakespeare, <u>King Henry V</u>

THE LAST DROP

Close every saloon, every
brewery; death to the seller,
or maker, (of beer).

General John J. Pershing (1860-1948)

THE CORRUPTION OF YOUTH

There are few acts more reprehensible than that of parents sending their children to the neighboring saloons for beer, or sadder sights than to see these little ones, who can hardly reach up to the top of the counter, buying beer, and then stopping in the street, as the writer has seen them do, to take a drink out of the pails and pitches of beer which they were carrying home.

Dominion Church of England Journal,
1887

But I tell you what — half the children who come here drink. That's how drunkards are made. Their mothers and fathers send 'em for beer. They see the old folks tipple, and begin to taste the beer themselves. Few of the children who come in here for beer or ale carry a full pint home...We must sell it, however, when their parents send for it... Business is business.

Interview with a bartender,
<u>New York Herald</u>, 1880

The beer drunkard is the worst drunkard in the world, and his chains are the heaviest and strongest.

Petroleum v. Nasby, circa 1880

BEER GOES TO MOVIES

"Care to join us in a glass of beer?"

Humphrey Bogart, as killer Duke Mantee
in "The Petrified Forest"

By the early nineteen-twenties and the advent of Prohibition, beer figured most often into Hollywood gangster fantasies; lurid visions of illicit breweries run by machine gun toting brewmasters and their scar-faced henchmen. At right is a highly selective list of movies with memorable beer moments or lines.

"Of Human Bondage," starring Bette
Davis and Leslie Howard, directed by
John Cromwell, 1934.

"The Deer Hunter," starring Robert De
Niro and Meryl Streep, directed by
Michael Cimino, 1978.

"The Lady Eve" starring Henry Fonda
and Barbara Stanwyck, directed by
Preston Sturges, 1941.

It's extraordinary how friendly you can make a lot of people on a couple bottles of beer.

Baron Frankenstein in "Frankenstein," directed by James Whale, 1931

THE PHILOSPHICAL DRINKER

And you say, said I, that the universe is really a vast pint of beer?
. . . They proceeded with the speed
of rockets to the northeast corner of
the universe, which George now per-
ceived to be shaped exactly like a
pint of beer, in which the nebulae
were the ascending bubbles.

John Colier,
The Devil, George and Rosie

When the beer
bubbles, the
masses forget
their troubles.

The People's Daily, Peking,
China, 1991

I think **fourty-nine**
Guinnesses is piggish.

Dylan Thomas

A LITERARY BREW

He went into an old taproom with a bare floor, spittoons, a pot-belly stove burning wood, and a droning congregation of old-timers drinking beer at the bar. He ordered a beer. An old man with white hair was there singing a song, holding a beer in one hand, waving his other hand with a firm, grave, completely un-selfconscious gesture of sincerity and pleased determination to sing. . . . Martin knew that some of these men had been drinking in this bar for almost half a century . . . drinking in this bar in the 1890's of New York when the beer wagons were drawn thundering over cobbles by massive horses. They had begun drinking here after their fathers, and their fathers had been drinking in this taproom in the 1840's of New York when the water-front streets were overspanned by jib-booms of ancient sailing ships. . . . He took off his hat and listened to the old man's song, and when it was over he bought the singer a beer and had it brought to him down the bar. They raised their glasses and drank to each other solemnly and respectful-ly across the room.

Jack Kerouac,
The Town and The City, 1950

O ales that were creamy like lather!
O beer that were foamy like suds!
O fizz that I love like a father —
O fie on the drinks that are duds!

Christopher Morley (1890-1957)

How much beer is in German intelligence?

Friedrich Nietzsche (1844-1900)

There is no
beverage which
I have liked to
live with more
than Beer.

George Saintsbury, 1920

Oh, I have been to Ludlow fair
And left my necktie God knows where,
And carried half way home, or near,
Pints and quarts of Ludlow beer.

A.E. Housman (1859-1936)

Happy the age and harmless
    were the days,
For then true love and
    amity were found,
When every village did a
    May-pole raise,
And Whitsun ales and May-
    games did abound.

                    Anonymous

COLONIAL LIFE

William Penn wrote in 1685 of his progress in the colony, "Our drink has been beer and punch, made of rum and water: Our beer was mostly made of molasses, which well boyld, with sassafras or pine infused into it, makes very tolerable drink; but now they make mault, and mault drink begins to be common, especially at the ordinaries and the houses of the more substantial people. In our great town there is an able man, that has set up a large brew house, in order to furnish the people with good drink, both there and up and down the river."

We must regain
our confidence
and struggle to
keep a perspec-
tive on the
present-day
judgments of the
beer effete.

Pure water is the best of
gifts that man to man can bring.
But who am I that I should have
the best of anything?
Let princes revel at the pump,
let peers with ponds make free,
...beer is good enough for me.

Lord Charles Neaves (1800-1876)

THE DRINK OF CHOICE

"What would you like to drink, sir?"
he asked, holding out the wine list.
Uncle John smiled villainously up at
him as he pushed away the book.
"Beer. You don't imagine I am going
to ruin my digestion drinking your
vinegar disguised as Chateau this and
Chateau that, do you? There pints of
bitter."

Ruthven Todd (1914-1978)

As good wine needs no bush,
so beer needs no excuse.
One should drink it because
it is pleasing to drink and
not because it contains any
specific number of calories
or because it is either
good or bad for you.

Anonymous, 1934

If you...want to take beer for the picnic or motor trip, resort to the old method of wrapping cold beer just out of the ice box in wet newspapers. It will stay cold for two hours.

Virginia Elliott, 1933

Beer is proof
that God loves
us and wants us
to be happy.

Benjamin Franklin (1706-1790)

THE PHILOSOPHICAL DRINKER

God did so love the world He/She bestowed upon women the secrets of beer making. Allowing His/Her children to share in the divine, joyous, and eternal, through tribal beer-drinking celebrations. Implicit in this gift was a test, a trial, a right of passage, a benchmark for social conduct, and a platform for politics among ancient and modern hunter-gatherers.

Beer is the most democratic and most feminine of all beverages.

COLLECTION REFLECTION

Linger here and live the past of
  armored storybooks amassed.
Hear the tales of hunt and chase that
  brought them to this resting place.
Each was once a frosty well that time
  has made a rusty shell
with messages inscribed upon that give
  a glimpse of time that's gone.

Drained of all fermented brews they're
  filled with only secret clues
of lives they touched with liquid
  gold and hidden tales ne'er to be
  told.
So ponder this peculiar sight partake
  of lager, dark or light
and muse upon these iron tombs
  embodied in the Beer Can Room.

Carrie Nation (1846-1911),
<u>Ax Grindings</u>

Mankind's joy
and saviour, a
true gift of
the gods, and,
above all else,
a drink with a
sense of humor
— this is Beer.

BEER'S BEGINNINGS

It is almost a universal human belief that beer did come into the world so that the sons and daughters of men might celebrate possessed by the spirit of the earth mother and forget the sorrows of death with the barley cup of forgetfulness that gladdens hearts in song and rejoicing.

Primordial beermakers could not have known the nutritious value in this mind-altering liquid. Beer was a valuable dietary boost at a time when wandering the land, eating whatever one could catch or gather, was a full-time, all-consuming, daily routine.

He is not deserving the
name of Englishman who
speaketh against ale, that
is, good ale.

George Borrow (1803-1881)

...What will bring the
   effervescence,
Who will add the needed
   factor,
That the beer may foam and
   sparkle,
May ferment and be
   delightful?

                    Kalevala, Rune #20

BEER ETIQUETTE

Norse ale was often
served with garlic added
as a charm to ward off
evil.

They told me this
story...while we were
waiting for an up-train. I
supplied the beer. The tale
was cheap at a gallon and a
half.

Rudyard Kipling (1865-1936)

RETURN OF THE HEATHER BREW

Commercial production of heather ale has recently resumed in Scotland.

Called "Leann fraoich" in Gaelic, sweet gale and flowering heather are added to boiling malted barley, the hot ale is then poured into a vat of fresh heather flowers where it infuses. While it is no longer made by Picts it still packs a punch.

During the Middle Ages, the word "ale" came to mean a fest, feast, or party. Beer-drinking to excess was the rule of the time.

GERMAN CUSTOM

In Germany, men spend most of the evening drinking beer and smoking with their friends, while the women-folk are by themselves...Those who sit at the table are called Beer Persons...Young and old drink beer, sing songs, make speeches, and in honour of one or the other they "rub a salamander." This is a curious ceremony of great antiquity. When the beer glasses are filled they are rubbed on the table; at the word of a command they are raised and emptied; and again on command every man rubs his glass on the table the second time, raises it and brings it down

with a crash. Anyone who brought his
glass down too early or too late
would spoil the salamander and be in
disgrace.

Mrs. Alfred Sidgwick,
<u>Home Life in Germany</u>, 1908

Today, many saints find themselves on beer bottles through no fault of their own. The majority of these holy men and women were neither patrons of beer nor even drinkers. Most of them got on a beer label through the custom of commercial monastic brewing.

I hear many cry when deplorable excesses happen, "Would there be no barley-wine!" Oh, folly! Oh, madness! Is it the ale that causes this abuse? No. It is the intemperance of those who take evil delight in it. Cry rather, "Would to God there were no drunkenness, no luxury."

John Chrysostom,
Greek Saint, 2nd century

THE LEGEND OF ST. ADRIAN

Saint Adrian is, perhaps the chief among saints of beer, recognized as such throughout the world. Saint Adrian's day, celebrated on the 8th of September is occasion for much Christian beer drinking in Europe.

The pre-saintly Adrian was a praetorian guard to the emperor Maximilian. Legend has it that one day, while overseeing the torturing of some Christians, Adrian became impressed with the fortitude of those being roasted. Adrian was so impressed he renounced the emperor, gave his soul to Jesus, and was promptly put to the sword in Nicomedia on 4 March 303 A.D.

Adrian, historians tell us, died in his wife's arms after having his own arms and head cut off. Mrs. Adrian soon followed Adrian to those pearly gates. Just how Adrian became associated with beer remains unclear.

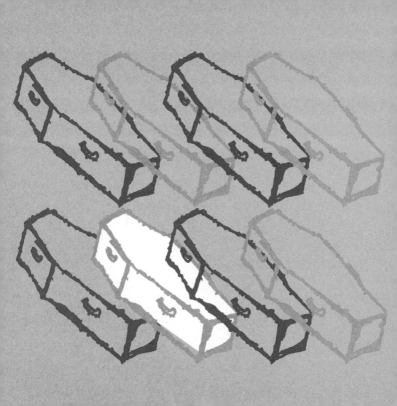

Funeral ales, accompanying celebrations for the dead and in memory of the departed, were a common feature of life that even survived to the colonies in the New World.

Mine host was full of ale
and history.

Richard Corbet (1582–1653), Poems

Iago:
To suckle fools
and chronicle
small beer.

William Shakespeare, <u>Othello</u>, Act I

And many a skeleton shook
   his head.
"Instead of preaching forty
   year!"
My neighbour Parson Thirdly
   said,
"I wish I had stuck to
   pipes and beer."

Thomas Hardy, <u>Channel Firing</u>, 1914

BEER ETIQUETTE

The champagne toast may be more common during today's nuptial festivities, but in ancient times beer was the beverage for bride and groom.

At first he wished to drink sherry, but I begged him to do no such thing...The landlord allowed himself to be dissuaded, and, after a glass or two of ale, confessed that sherry was a sickly, disagreeable drink...

George Borrow (1803–1881)

...It is indeed good beer;
and when we leave our val-
leys we will all drink it
together in paradise.

> Hilaire Belloc (1870—1953),
> <u>The Four Men</u>

BEER AND SONG

Why
Should I
Weep, wail, or sigh?
What if luck has passed me by?
What if my hopes are dead,
My pleasures fled?
Have I not still
My fill
Of right good cheer,
Cigars and beer?

George Arnold (1834–1865)

The best and brounest ale that brewsters sellen.

Robert Longlande,
Vision of Piers Plowman, 1377

In Valhalla, the heavenly ale-house of Viking myth, table service will be provided by the statuesque Valkyries — each more blonde and beautiful than the next.

The foam rises in the glass, trembles up, slops over. The barkeep cuts across the top with a wooden scoop, lets the foam settle a second, then puts the glass under the faintly wheezing spigot again...

John Dos Passos, 1925

WHY BEER?

One warm seacoast afternoon, I fell in love with beer. The tiny, six-ounce, jewel-green glass bottles held a strong, bitter, spruce forest taste that moved me. My life changed forever. My fate was sealed. That first soft kiss of malt and hops against my lips was my first step into a world I couldn't imagine then, a journey that would take me, beer glass in hand, to some of the least traveled, most remote places on earth. From desert tombs to jungle tribes, I was always in quest of the spirit and soul of beer, the secret life and true meaning of beer.